We Like to Nurse Too

Mary Young

Design by Zachary Parker

World Health Series

HOHM PRESS
Chino Valley, Arizona

For Lee and for nursing babies everywhere.

© 2009 Mary Young

Cover design, interior layout and design: Zac Parker, Kadak Graphics, Prescott, AZ.
Illustration design by Zachary Parker (some elements from stock sources).

Library of Congress Cataloging-in-Publication Data

Young, Mary.
We like to nurse too / Mary Young ; illustrated by Zachary Parker.
    p. cm.
ISBN 978-1-890772-98-7 (trade paper : alk. paper)
1. Marine mammals--Infancy--Juvenile literature. 2. Breastfeeding--Juvenile literature. I. Parker, Zac. II. Title.
QL713.2.Y68 2009
599.5'139--dc22
                        2009009156

HOHM PRESS
P.O. Box 4410, Chino Valley, AZ 86323
800-381-2700 • www.hohmpress.com

This book was printed in China.

We Like to Nurse and *We Like to Nurse Too* promote the importance of infant breastfeeding while drawing attention to our kinship with all mammals. In *We Like to Nurse Too* we focus on sea mammals living in the oceans of this beautiful planet we share as home. "People protect what they love," said Jacques Cousteau, the great oceanographer. Today, the ocean environment is threatened by pollution and debris dumped into the oceans, melting polar ice caps, and by hunters. Careful decisions made by humans can save our planet; we believe that introducing young children to the nursing activity of animals can foster a love and concern that will grow to protect the planet we love.

Sea lion babies like to roll
in the sand and snuggle up
to mamma while they nurse.

Mamma dolphin rolls on her side
to make it easy for her baby to nurse.
Dolphins are a kind of whale.

Humpback whale mothers squirt thick creamy milk into the mouths of their calves. Did you know that humpback whales sing?

Seal pups nurse and play
with their mothers at sunset.

Walrus calves nurse upside down while they float in the water. When they play, the mother holds the calf in her flipper fins and lifts it into the air!

Seals, sea lions and walruses are sea mammals called pinnepeds (PIN-A-PEDS). They use their flipper fins to swim in clear ocean water.

Porpoise pup nurses with her mother in a harbor river.

Baby narwhal nurses with his mother in cold icy water.

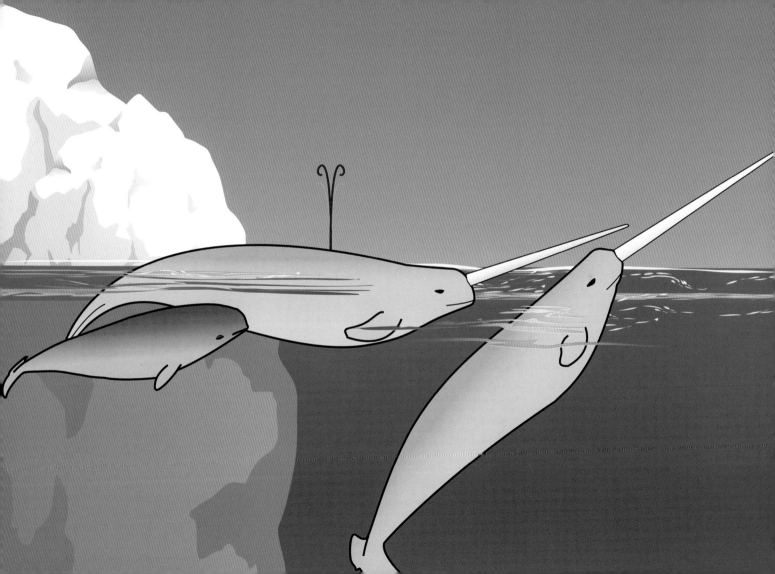

Polar bear cubs nurse in dens of ice and snow made by their mothers.

Manatee calves and mothers call to each other and nurse under the water.

Sea otter mamma hugs her pup affectionately while they nurse.

Noisy elephant seal pups shout for their milk on the sandy beach.

A newborn orca whale calf is bigger than a full-grown person. They nurse while they glide under the surface of the ocean.

We like to nurse too!

OTHER TITLES IN HOHM PRESS' FAMILY HEALTH & WORLD HEALTH SERIES

We Like To Nurse
by Chia Martin
Illustrations by Shukyo Rainey
Captivating illustrations present mother animals nursing their young, and honors the mother-child bond created by nursing.

ISBN: 978-1-934252-45-4, paper, 32 pages, $9.95
Spanish Language Version: *Nos Gusta Amamanatar*
ISBN: 978-1-890772-41-3

Breastfeeding:
Your Priceless Gift to
Your Baby and Yourself
by Regina Sara Ryan and
Deborah Auletta, RN, IBCLC
Pleads the case for breastfeeding as the healthiest option for both baby and mom with gorgeous photos and 20 compelling reasons why breastfeeding is best.
ISBN: 978-1-890772-48-2, paper, 32 pages, $9.95.
Spanish Language Version: *Amamantar* ISBN: 978-1-890772-57-4

We Like to Live Green
by Mary Young
Colorful photo montages introduce vital environmental themes to both young children and adults. This helpful book suggests how we can all make a difference in our world threatened by ecological crises.

ISBN: 978-1-935387-00-8, paper, 32 pages, $9.95
Bi-Lingual [English/Spanish] Version: *Nos Gusta Vivir Verde*
ISBN: 978-1-935387-01-5

We Like to Play Music
by Kate Parker
An easy-to-read picture book full of photographs of children playing music, moving to a beat and enjoying music alone and with others. The rhyming text says how everyone can shake a rattle, dance to a beat, or even form their own "band."
ISBN: 978-1-890772-85-7, paper, 32 pages, $9.95.
Bi-Lingual [English/Spanish] Version: *Nos Gusta Tocar Música*
ISBN: 978-1-890772-90-1

TO ORDER: *800-381-2700, or visit our website, www.hohmpress.com *Special discounts for bulk orders.*